French Fries Up Your Nose

ALDEN NUSSER is thirteen years old, lives in Manhattan, and shares his home with his parents and a couple of mice who live under the dishwashing machine.

French Fries Up Your Nose

208 WAYS TO ANNOY PEOPLE

Alden Nusser

Illustrated by Paul Brewer

FRENCH FRIES UP YOUR NOSE is an original publication of Avon Books. This work has never before appeared in book form.

AVON BOOKS
A division of
The Hearst Corporation
1350 Avenue of the Americas
New York, New York 10019

Interior illustrations by Paul Brewer
Published by arrangement with the author
Library of Congress Catalog Card Number: 95-6192
ISBN: 0-380-78372-X

Library of Congress Cataloging in Publication Data:
Nusser, Alden.
French fries up your nose: 208 ways to annoy people / Alden Nusser.
pp. cm.—(An Avon Camelot book)
Summary: Presents suggestions for annoying other people, arranged in such categories as "Bathroom Behavior," "Eating Habits," and "Telephone Tricks."
1. Wit and humor, Juvenile. [1. Wit and humor.] I. Title.
PN6163.N87 1995 95-6192
818'.5402—dc20 CIP
AC

First Avon Camelot Printing: August 1995

Printed in the U.S.A.

OPM 10 9 8 7 6 5 4 3 2 1

CONTENTS

PLACES TO ANNOY PEOPLE

WAYS TO ANNOY PEOPLE WHO ANNOY YOU

AUTHOR'S NOTE

Warning:
Annoying people can be addictive.

PREFACE

Most guide books are written to bring out the best in you. This book is unique, because it is written to bring out your worst. Why? Just because it's fun. Even the biggest goody-two-shoes will admit that it's fun to think of the science teacher's chronic diarrhea acting up due to a commotion that you have provoked.

Everybody has an innate ability to be annoying. This book will strengthen the pleasurable gift you have to make people moan, groan, flinch, yell, and squirm.

I am interested in collecting new and exciting annoyances (possibly for another book, or just to make myself even more irritating than I already am). You can send them to me: Mr. Annoyance, c/o Avon Books, 1350 Avenue of the Americas, New York, New York 10019.

Also send money in the event I am sent to court due to a hazardous annoyance.

French Fries Up Your Nose

OPPORTUNITIES TO ANNOY PEOPLE

1
BATHROOM BEHAVIOR

Hide in the shower, wait until your dad is ready to climb in, and frighten him.

Leave the toilet seat up.

Wash your hair in the toilet.

Spit in the sink and don't rinse it out.

Drink some bath water.

Place a couple of feet of toilet paper into the bowl without tearing it off the roll. Then flush. Watch the toilet devour it. Bonus: It may clog the toilet.

Hide your father's Maalox.

Discharge the entire can of potpourri spray.

Forget to flush.

2
FUN WITH THE FAMILY

Shoot your father in the back of the head with your rubber band gun. Aim for the bald spot.

Jump on the bed.

Jump on the couch.

Complain that you're bored.

Careen yourself down a flight of steps.
Complain that it hurt.

When there is a fight, joyously start singing the theme to "Family Feud."

Always blame everything on someone else.

3
SHOPPING

Refuse to try on clothes in the store. Insist on bringing them home first.

Don't be interested in buying anything except another T-shirt.

Let your mother buy whatever it is she thinks you should have but express no interest or opinion. Do not ever wear these clothes.

When your mother takes something out of your closet and says she is going to throw it away because it is worn out and/or disgusting looking, even if you haven't worn it in months, get interested in wearing it again.

Ask the clerk in the store how much 27 different salt shakers cost. Then ask about another one. Then ask about another one, and another one, and another one . . . then don't buy any.

Say all the sneakers feel bad except the ones that cost $125.

Pull the tag off your new pants, put them on, and then say that they felt okay in the store but now they don't feel right.

Once you've worn them, tell your parents that the $125 sneakers don't feel right either.

Beg for a catcher's mitt until your parents spend $75 on it, and after they buy it decide you're no good as a catcher and want to play first base.

Beg for a video game and say you won't spend all your time with it. The first night you get it home keep sneaking away from your homework to play the video game so they have to keep calling you back to finish your homework.

4
EATING HABITS

Always swig from the carton.

Take a swig from the carton while your mother is talking on the phone to her boss (hoping that she will scream and sound like a fool).

Put blue food coloring in water and pretend you're drinking Windex.

Taste a dog biscuit and tell everyone it's delicious. Bark.

Ask what's for dinner and, no matter what the answer is, complain, "Not that again!"

Say you're starved, ask what's for dinner, and then say, "I'm not hungry." Don't eat. An hour later, say you're hungry.

5
TELEPHONE TRICKS

Try to interrupt your mother the minute she starts talking on the phone. When she's off the phone and asks what you wanted, say you forgot.

Keep hanging up when you're on a call with your grandmother and say it must be a bad connection.

Pretend you're receiving the call you just placed. Example:

You: "Hello?"
Them: "Hello?"
You: "Hello?"
Them: "Hello?"
You: "Helloooooo? Who's calling, please?"

Take a cap gun and call someone.
When they answer, shoot it and scream.
Then hang up.

Remain in the bathroom while your grandmother is calling for you.

Play "Dick Van Dyke" reruns to your grandmother.

6
AT THE TABLE

Take a tomato and announce its name is Tommy Tomato and he's not feeling too well. Squeeze it.

Put barbecue sauce on everything, including your bread.

Put barbecue sauce in your water.

Put your face in the plate and suck up all the peas with your nose.

Spin spaghetti like a lasso.

Gut the bread.

While you are at the dinner table, say you think you have worms.

7
PLAYING WITH YOUR PET

Beg for a pet, say you'll take care of it and do anything for it, and when you get it leave the job up to your parents.

Train your cat to use a hula hoop.

Dye your dog's hair.

Try to lick yourself clean like a cat.

Pick up your hamster and put it down and pick it up and put it down and pick it up and put it down.

When your mother says that you're picking up the hamster and putting it down too many times, first say you are not and then tell her the hamster likes it.

When your lizard or turtle dies, put it away in your closet and forget about it. When someone asks, "What's that funny odor?" act clueless.

8
RESPONDING TO DISCIPLINE

When your mom is on the phone and waving at you to keep quiet, look at her as if you don't understand what she's doing.

When your parents tell you not to play with balls inside the house, say you won't break anything and believe that saying that makes it so.

When your parents tell you that you can't watch your favorite TV show because you didn't do something they asked you to do, say you never heard them ask.

Whenever you are asked to do something, complain it's not fair.

9

FUN WITH YOUR BODY

Stick strips of straw wrapper up your nose and snort them out. Yell at your parents when they say you'll get one stuck. Get one stuck.

Bite your toenails.

Pick a scab.

Shoot rubber bands from your braces.

Make gassy sounds.

Belch.

Try to open an oyster inside your elbow.

Mousse your hair into a punk-do on a religious holiday.

10
WHEN YOU'RE BORED

Use up all the rubber cement making rubber balls.

Click a ball-point pen repeatedly.

Order Cinemax while your parents are asleep.

Start a food fight.

Pull someone's pants down.

11
DOING HOMEWORK

Leave your homework at school. Remember that you left it there just as you were about to go to sleep. Get very upset. Provoke a fight between your mother and father about why you are so disorganized. Don't forget: Sing the "Family Feud" song.

At 10 p.m. announce to your mother that you have to bring a Pilgrim dish for the Thanksgiving feast tomorrow morning.

At 10 p.m. announce to your mother that you have to do a research project on Cyrus of Persia that's due in the morning. Be very upset when she doesn't have a reference book that has information on him.

Instead of doing your homework, practice making unusual faces in the mirror.

Spill things on your friends' homework at lunch.

12
ATTENTION-GETTERS

Vote against any pizza topping except cheese.

Spit out bologna.

Pretend you are a dog and try to whiz.

When someone asks you what a movie is about, start at the very beginning and tell them the complete story. Keep remembering parts you forgot and start all over again. Get angry when you're interrupted.

PLACES TO ANNOY PEOPLE

13
IN THE MALL

Go down the up escalator.

Go up the down escalator.

Take a ride in the revolving door.

Put a bra on your head and announce, "It fits."

Ask how much 13 different windproof lighters cost. Leave.

Eat the whole plate of samples. Leave.

Complain about the smell of the store to the manager.

14
AT THE MOVIES

Spill the popcorn.

Insist on having the giant-size soda, drink it all before the previews are over, and go to the bathroom at least three or four times. Each time you come back, make someone tell you what you missed.

Lose something under the seat (especially if the floor is very, very sticky and your parent has to get on his hands and knees to find it).

When you get home, suddenly remember that you have lost something under the seat.

Put peanut M&Ms in the hood of the person in front of you.

Put peanut M&Ms down the back of the person in front of you.

15
ON A CAR TRIP

Spit out the window.

Spit at the window.

Make vomiting noises from the back seat.

Vomit.

Refuse to go to the bathroom when everyone else goes to the bathroom at the rest stop.

Wait until one exit after the rest stop (or until you see the sign announcing the next rest stop is 27 miles away) and announce you have to go to the bathroom right away.

Refuse to go to the bathroom in a plastic cup that your mother has brought along for this purpose. Keep clutching your stomach, saying "I have to GO!" and continue to make everyone in the car uncomfortable.

Move the rear view mirror when the driver leaves the car.

Turn on every function—radio, AC, radar detector, fan—when the driver is in the bathroom.

16
IN A RESTAURANT

Inquire about every beverage on the menu. Decide on water.

Order an omelet and don't eat it when it comes with parsley on top.

Order a cheeseburger and say the cheese smells funny and you can't eat it.

Knock anything over.

Put a napkin on your head and say you're a nun.

Drench your french fries with vinegar before anyone can take any. When anyone complains, say you like them that way.

Design an interesting drum solo on the table.

Mix all the liquids, salt, pepper, ketchup, and whatever else you can find in one glass.

Mix all the liquids, salt, pepper, ketchup, and whatever else you can find in one glass. Knock the glass over.

Keep tipping your chair until it is on the verge of rolling over.

Ask for the wine menu.

17
AT THE BEACH

Complain that the sand is too hot and the water is too cold.

Trip on the little kids' sand castles.

Get sand into the sunscreen lotion.

Bury your sister until she screams.

Bury your brother's beach toys. Be unable to find them.

Carry two drinks all the way from the concession stand to the blanket, put them down, sit down, and knock one drink over. Say it was your sister's drink and be completely unwilling to share the one you're drinking. Gulp it down before your parents can force you to share it.

Carry two drinks all the way from the concession stand to the blanket, put them down, sit down, and knock both drinks over. Cry or whine (depending on your age) until your parents go get another one.

18
AWAY AT CAMP

Keep stealing your counselor's underwear.

Short-sheet the counselor's bed.

Read aloud the counselor's mail from his girlfriend. Make loud smacking noises at the sappy parts.

Steal the counselor's food.

Steal someone else's bed and make yourself a queen-size one.

Write home and just say, "Camp is great. I love you. Bye."

Write home and say, "The food here is better than at home."

Don't write home.

19
ELEVATOR BEHAVIOR

Press every floor before you get out.

Hang on the grab bars in the elevator. When your parents tell you the bars will break say, "No, they won't."

Leave chewed gum on an elevator button.

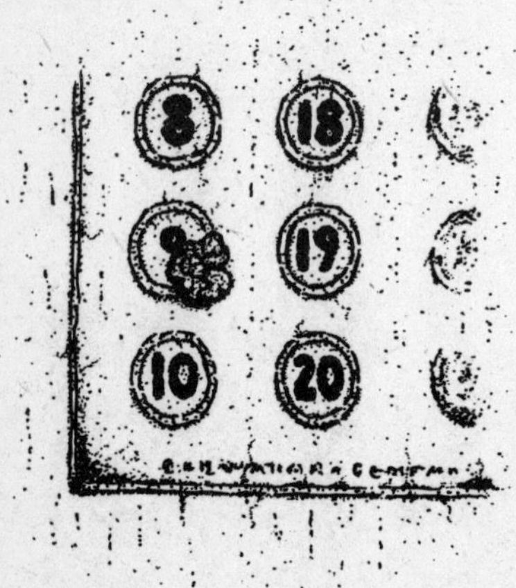

Leave anything undesirable on an elevator button.

In a crowded elevator loudly announce, "I feel very gassy."

20
IN RELIGIOUS SCHOOL

Ask the teacher, "What really happens when you die?" Find every answer unsatisfactory.

Announce that you're thinking of converting.

Find a disaster in the news. Ask the teacher, "If there is a God, why did He do that?"

21
AT THE DOCTOR'S OFFICE

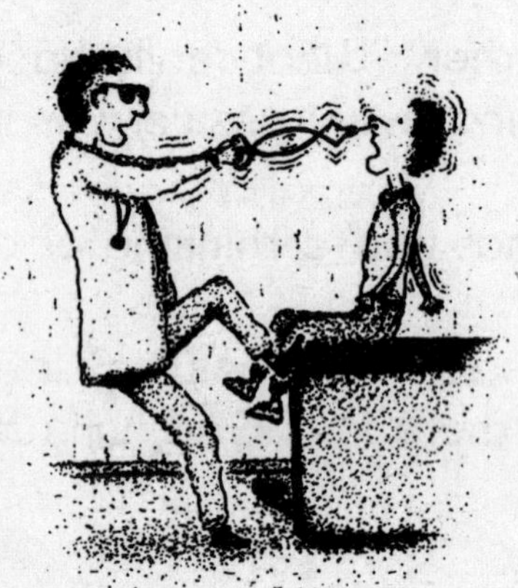

Take a Q-Tip from the jar, stick it up your nose, and tell the doctor it's stuck.

Switch folders so the doctor thinks you're next.

Try to weigh yourself on the baby scale.

Monopolize the rocking turtle.

Infect everything.

22
VISITING THE DENTIST

Pick up all the things in the tray to look at them.

Spray water.

Move your tongue in front of the places where the dentist wants to work.

Try to locate your brain with the little mirror, via your nose.

Ask if it will hurt. Ask again. And again. And again.

23
AT THE BARBER'S

Pump all the chairs up and down while you are waiting for your turn.

Put a straw in the Barbicide and pretend to drink it.

Insist on wearing your Walkman during the haircut. Move to the music.

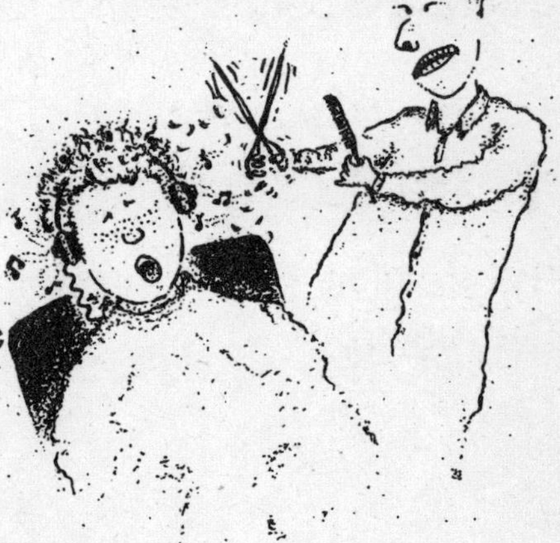

Pretend you have a nervous twitch in the barber's chair.

Play with the electric razor.

Insist on drinking a milkshake during the haircut. Complain when a hair gets in it.

Find something very interesting to do with your shoelaces when the barber is trimming the nape of your neck.

24
TRAVELING BY AIR

Desperately require something in the overhead bin the minute everyone has settled in.

Explain to the person sitting next to you that you are a representative of the Hare Krishna and ask for a donation.

Keep slamming the tray.

Repeatedly push the button to call the stewardess.

Lose the headset in the middle of the movie. Grovel for another one.

Recline all the way. Sit up. Recline. Sit up. Recline. Sit up . . .

25
AT AN AMUSEMENT PARK

Turn the go cart into a bumper ride.

Pretend your cart has no brakes.

Spit straight up in the air on the roller coaster and hope to hit the person behind you.

Eat right before you go on the "Nausearama" ride.

Tell younger children there is a 40 percent chance they'll get run over during the Bambi ride.

Drop your hat in a slow flume ride. Insist on getting it back.

WAYS TO ANNOY PEOPLE WHO ANNOY YOU

26
YOUNGER CHILDREN

Teach them bad words and tell them they're nice words and to scream the words out so your grandmother, who can't hear very well, will be sure to hear them.

Whenever they are about to tell the punch line of a joke, scream it out.

Tickle them until they start hiccuping and/or get nauseous.

Tell your sister if she puts her hand all the way into the toilet, she'll find something. Tell her if there is nothing to be found, flush.

Tell them they were adopted.

Persuade them to spend their allowance on fake dog doody.

Draw on them. Use permanent marker. (Don't worry; it will wash off—eventually.)

Hold their toys ransom.

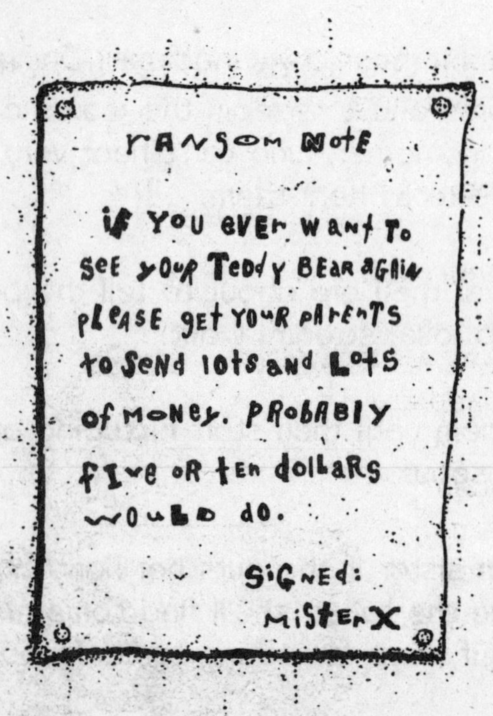

27
OLDER SIBLINGS

Collect snow from the windowsill. Dump it on your sleeping sister.

Eavesdrop.

Open their mail.

Tease your older brother about pimples.

"Trim" your brother's or sister's hair while they're napping.

28
YOUR CLASSMATES

Tell the class nerd that the most popular girl in the class secretly loves him.

Get the class overachiever worked up about a fictitious report due tomorrow.

Nickname your classmates personally. For example, you like the name Barry. . . .

Call all your classmates and say, "I'm on the committee to remind you that we're supposed to wear swimsuits and sandals to school tomorrow."

Ask if your classmate meant to eat the hair that was on her school lunch.

29
YOUR TEACHER

Pretend that you are speaking by just moving your lips so the teacher has to say, "Speak up."

Work up a good imitation of your teacher. Do it whenever his back is turned. When he asks what's funny, say you don't know.

When you are on a class trip, hide from the teacher.

Every time the teacher leaves the room, follow.

Correct the teacher's corrections.

30
THE SUBSTITUTE

Hide the instructions.

Swear that every boy in the class is named Barry.

Swear that every girl in the class is named Barry.

Talk about how stupid the last substitute was.

Ask the substitute how old he is. Ask if he has kids. Ask how much he's getting paid. Ask. Ask. Ask.

31
YOUR MUSIC TEACHER

Forget to practice.

Say your instrument went out of tune the day after the lesson and you didn't know how to tune it.

Announce you've gotten very good at playing the piano with your head and say you'd like to demonstrate.

When you start to practice, say your fingers/head/arm hurt(s).

Tell your teacher you know the theme to Lé Buttéchícs (butt cheeks) and sing while compressing your butt cheeks with your hands. When your teacher gets mad, say she has an old person's sense of humor.

32
YOUR MOM

Call your mom, and call her again and again and again and again and again. When she comes into the room, say, "Never mind."

Start reading at bedtime. When your mom tells you to go to sleep, say she's ruining your educational motivation.

Before you leave the house in the morning, write in lipstick on her mirror, "I HAVE YOUR SON."

Drop your clothes on the floor.

Don't remember to give your mom any of the flyers that they send home from school.

Tell your mom she has a big hair on her chin.

Ask your mom how old she is in an elevator. Be shocked when she gives you the answer. Say she said she was older last week.

33
YOUR DAD

Tell him your grandmother told you he was adopted.

Answer your dad's business phone and explain that the caller has reached the Star of India restaurant.

Draw mustaches on everybody in your dad's magazines.

Gather a group of friends to admire your dad's snoring.

Lose the TV clicker.